Food

Peter Chrisp

Wayland

Titles in the series

Country Life

Exploration

Food

Kings and Queens

Homes

Religion

Scientists and Writers

Town Life

Cover illustrations: *Background*: The Tabard Inn, London, in 1490.
Inset: A noble family dining in the late seventeenth century.

First published in 1994 by Wayland (Publishers) Ltd
61 Western Road, Hove, East Sussex, BN3 1JD, England

© Copyright 1994 Wayland (Publishers) Ltd

Series editor: Cath Senker
Book editor: Katie Roden
Designer: John Christopher
Picture researcher: Elizabeth Moore

British Library Cataloguing in Publication Data
Chrisp, Peter
Food. – (Tudors and Stuarts series)
I. Title II. Series
641.309
ISBN 0-7502-1111-3

Typeset by Strong Silent Type
Printed and bound by B.P.C.C. Paulton Books, Great Britain

Notes for teachers

Food contains a wide range of exciting sources including contemporary artefacts, paintings, quotations and drawings.

This book:

◆ describes the diets and eating habits of Tudor and Stuart people from across the social spectrum;

◆ shows how food in Scotland, Wales and Ireland differed from the English diet;

◆ shows how the many voyages of exploration introduced new foods to Britain;

◆ helps the reader to understand how we use clues from the past to learn about how people lived then.

Picture acknowledgements
Ancient Art and Architecture Collection 25; Aviemore Photographic 8; Bibliothèque royale Albert 1er, Brussels 12; Bridgeman Art Library *cover* (inset), 5, 7, 10, 13 (top), 17 (top), 21 (top); Cadbury Ltd 27 (bottom); Robert Estall 22; E.T. archive 6 (both), 19 (bottom); Mary Evans Picture Library 9, 18, 20; Fotomas Index 13 (bottom), 14, 16, 23 (bottom), 24 (top); Michael Holford 19 (top), 27 (top); Hulton Picture Library 23 (top); Image Select (Ann Ronan) 17 (bottom); J R Moore 4, 21 (bottom); National Portrait Gallery 15, 24 (bottom); Wayland Picture Library *cover* (background), 11.

Contents

In the 1500s

This book is about the food that people in Britain ate during the time of the Tudor and Stuart kings and queens. The Tudors ruled over England and Wales from 1485 to 1603. The Stuarts, who also ruled Scotland, were on the throne from 1603 to 1714.

When the Tudors first came to power, British food was very different from the food we eat today. Many things we now take for granted, such as potatoes and tomatoes, were unknown. King Henry VII, the first Tudor king, never ate any of the foods in the picture on the left. Henry would not even have known that these *were* foods. If you had offered him a potato, he would not have known what it was for!

Today we can eat food from all over the world. In Henry's time, people only ate food from plants that they could grow locally. Their meat came from animals that they looked after or hunted. Nowadays, we can flavour our food with lots of different spices – such as pepper, ginger, coriander and cumin – grown in distant lands. In Henry's time, only the richest people could afford any of these spices.

All these foods were discovered by Europeans in the 1500s.

This picture, by the Flemish painter Pieter Brueghel the Younger, shows a man drinking ale with his food. Everyone in Britain drank ale with their meals.

There were no hot drinks like tea or coffee and hardly any soft drinks. Most people refused to drink water. Towns were filthy places and the water was usually too dirty to drink. Instead of water, everyone, even tiny children, drank ale. A doctor called Andrew Borde wrote:

"Water is not wholesome by itself for an Englishman. I myself, who am a physician, avoid water and take myself to good ale."

During the time of the Tudors and Stuarts, people learned about many new kinds of food and drink. Gradually, the food people ate in Britain began to change.

The yearly routine

Nowadays, we can eat almost any food at any time of the year. During Tudor times, people's food changed from season to season. In the summer and autumn there was usually plenty of fresh food, but this ran out when the winter came. In winter, there was not enough food to keep all the farm animals alive. Most of them were killed in the autumn, before they started losing weight.

This picture shows a man cutting wheat at the August harvest.

This French picture from the mid fifteenth century shows a man sowing wheat that will grow through the winter.

The changing pattern of the farming year can be seen in the pictures on this page. They show the work that had to be done on the farm at different times of the year. You can tell the time of year from the signs of the zodiac.

There were no fridges, so the meat from animals was salted, pickled or smoked to stop it going rotten. In the winter months, people lived on the salted meat and on dried foods such as beans, peas and lentils.

The animals which were kept alive through the winter had very little to eat. According to a poet called Thomas Tusser:

> *"From Christmas till May be well entered in, Cattle grow faint and look poorly and thin."*

Religion controlled the sort of food you could eat at different times of the year. British people were almost all Christians and the Church had lots of rules about eating. Eating meat was banned on certain days, called 'fish days' or 'fast days'.

These were every Friday and Saturday, the forty days before Easter (Lent), and the four weeks before Christmas.

There were also religious 'holy days' when people were allowed to eat and drink as much as they liked. Holy days were Sundays, Easter Day, Christmas Day and important saints' days. On holy days, people didn't work – this is where the word 'holidays' comes from. After going to church, they would spend the rest of the day drinking, dancing and playing games, as in the painting below.

This sixteenth-century painting by Pieter Brueghel the Elder shows a saint's day celebration.

Scotland, Ireland and Wales

The north and west of the British Isles are much colder and wetter than the south. Crops like wheat, which do well in England, do not grow easily in Scotland. Instead of growing wheat, the Scots grew oats, which love cool, wet places. The English looked down on oats, because they didn't make good bread. However, the Scots found lots of ways of eating them. The best-known way was as porridge – oats mixed with salt and milk. Oats were also mixed with butter to make a dish called *brose*, mixed with cheese to make *brochan* and with water as *crowdie*.

In hilly areas like the Scottish Highlands, it was easier to keep cattle than to grow crops. As a result, the Scots drank much more milk than the English. Their small, tough cattle did well on the wet, windswept hillsides. The cattle's shaggy hair kept them warm and they needed less food than bigger animals.

Cattle were also important in Ireland. English visitors to Ireland thought that the Irish were backward people who didn't know the right way to live. This is what one Englishman, Fynes Morison, wrote:

> "As for the cheese or butter made by the Irish, an Englishman would not touch it with his lips...The wild Irish are most filthy in their diet...They have neither beer nor ale, but drink milk, warmed with a stone first cast into a fire."

A Highland cow.

An Irish feast in 1581.

Above is an English picture of an Irish feast, held in the open air. Instead of a metal pot, the Irish are cooking their meat in an animal skin, stretched over a fire. The picture was meant to show that Irish people were strange and funny.

The Welsh kept goats and sheep, using their milk for butter and cheese.

They loved to toast hard lumps of cheese in front of a fire – a special treat that became known as 'Welsh Rarebit'. The Welsh also ate lots of oats. They mixed them with milk or water and made them into oatcakes called *bara ceirch*. These were baked on a flat stone which had been heated on a fire. On page 30 you will find a recipe for Welsh oatcakes.

Three meals a day

A wealthy family saying grace before a meal, in 1602.

In Tudor and Stuart times, people got up and went to bed much earlier than we do today. They were up at about five or six o'clock in the morning and usually asleep by nine o'clock at night. This was because they only had candles or rushlights (straw burning in dishes of animal fat) to light their homes. Without good lighting, people had no reason to stay up late. It made much more sense for them to be up and about when there was daylight.

The first thing people did when they rose was to say their prayers. Then they might have had a light breakfast of ale and bread, but many people did not eat at all when they first got up.

The main meal was dinner, taken between eleven in the morning and midday. In the painting on the left you can see a family getting ready to eat their dinner. Do you know why their hands are clasped? They are saying 'grace', a short prayer to thank God for their meal. This is one grace that people said:

*"O Lord, who give thy creatures
for our food,
Herbs, beasts, birds, fish, and
other gifts of thine,
Bless these thy gifts, that they
may do us good,
And we may live, to praise
thy name divine. "*

The third meal of the day was supper, eaten between five and six o'clock in the evening. Supper was usually much lighter than dinner. It was often just bread, cheese and ale. Only very rich people had big meals at supper time.

A Stuart family at the supper table. They are eating bowls of meat and pieces of black bread.

The food of the poor

Poor people ate very simple food, usually bread or 'pottage', a sort of stew or soup made from beans, peas and any other cheap foods they could find. They grew vegetables, such as onions, cabbages and turnips, in the gardens of their cottages and kept hens for their eggs.

Poor people rarely ate meat. When they did eat meat, it was usually pork. They kept pigs, which were much smaller than today's pigs. These were easy to look after, as they could be fed on acorns and kitchen scraps.

All British people, rich and poor, ate lots of bread. However, there were big differences in the kinds of bread that were eaten. A writer called William Harrison described the sort of bread eaten by the poor:

© Bibliothèque royale Albert 1er, Bruxelles (Cabinet des Estampes).

> *While the gentlefolk provide themselves with wheat bread, their poor neighbours are forced to content themselves with rye or barley, yea, and in time of shortage, many with bread made either of beans, peas, or oats, or all these and some acorns among them.*

The Thin Kitchen by Pieter Brueghel the Elder.

A wedding feast, painted in 1568.

There was often not enough food, even in a good year. The winter was the worst time. People fell ill from diseases such as scurvy, as they could not get enough fresh food.

It was only on special occasions, such as this wedding feast in the picture above, that poor people could have a lot to eat. Most of the time, they had very little. In Pieter Brueghel the Elder's engraving, *The Thin Kitchen* (left), all the poor people are very thin, except for the man in the doorway. He looks like he is trying very hard to leave the cottage.

A beggar asking for money from a rich man.

In a bad year people could starve. In the 1590s, there were five bad years in a row. The weather was so wet that rivers flooded and the crops rotted in the fields. Many poor people died of hunger, or had to go out begging for money and food, as in the picture above.

The food of the rich

Rich people's food was very different from that of poor people. Rich people did not like vegetables, for example. They said that vegetables were bad for you because they made you 'windy'. What they liked was lots and lots of meat.

Elizabeth I on a picnic during a hunt in 1575.

Much of their meat came from hunting, the most popular sport for the wealthy. Henry VIII loved to hunt stags on horseback. Even when he was a sick old man, he would be lifted on to his horse by ropes and pulleys. He would ride off and watch the younger people chasing the stags.

In the picture on the left, rich people have stopped for a picnic during a hunt. It looks like they're going to be eating lots of roasted birds.

Rich people held great feasts during which many different dishes were served. You weren't expected to eat everything that was placed in front of you. It was more like a modern buffet, where you could choose particular dishes.

A lot of leftovers were given to the poor, who waited at the gates, begging.

A feast held by Sir Henry Unton, 1596.

Look at the picture of the feast held by Sir Henry Unton (above), with entertainment provided by actors and musicians. Compare this with the poor people's feast on page 13.

Kings and queens held feasts to show off their wealth and good taste – especially to impress foreign visitors. One such visitor was the ambassador from Venice, in what is now Italy. In 1517, he went to a feast held by Henry VIII. The meal lasted seven hours and there were ten courses. Musicians played all through the meal. The ambassador wrote:

" Every imaginable sort of meat known in the kingdom was served, and fish too, including prawn pasties of perhaps twenty different kinds, made in the shape of castles, and of animals of various kinds, as beautiful as can be imagined. In short, the wealth and civilization of the world are here. "

In the kitchen

Tudor kitchens were hot and smoky places, for food had to be cooked over an open fire. Cooks usually smelt of smoke from the fire and grease from the roasting meat. They had to work very hard. Today we have many gadgets to make cooking easier, but Tudor cooks had to do almost everything by hand.

In the picture below you can see how the fire was used. Some food is cooking in a pot hanging above the flames. There are ducks roasting on long pieces of metal called spits. Fat from the ducks collects in metal trays below the spits. The cook on the left is pouring this fat over the birds to stop them drying up.

Tudor cooks preparing a meal.

The spit had to be kept turning so that the meat cooked evenly. In this kitchen, the spit is being turned by a device with a slowly falling weight, but often a young boy or girl would have to sit by the fire turning a handle, as in the kitchen on the right. Some people even used dog power! A dog was trained to run inside a wheel which turned the spit.

When we cook something nowadays, we can turn up the heat with a knob on a cooker. You cannot do that with an open fire. If you want to increase the heat, you have to move your pot nearer to the flames. Cooks could do this in Tudor times by using a piece of metal called a 'ratchet hanger'. You can see pots hanging from ratchet hangers in the pictures.

Tudor cooks also had brick ovens for baking. A fire was burned in the oven until the bricks heated up. Then bread or pies were pushed in and baked by the heat from the bricks.

The pot in this kitchen above, painted by Pieter Brueghel the Elder, is held by a ratchet hanger.

Children are turning the spit in this kitchen.

At the table

Until the 1500s, people had very little tableware. Instead of plates, people ate from slices of stale bread called 'trenchers'. Even rich people used trenchers, as you can see in the picture below. In the 1500s, people stopped using bread, and began to eat from square pieces of wood, still called 'trenchers'. Richer people began to use plates.

Poor people ate their pottage from wooden bowls, with wooden spoons. They drank their ale from mugs made of wood or clay.

Richer people ate from dishes made of pewter. The richest people had silver plates and golden goblets. In this 1560s painting (right) of Lord Cobham and his family at the table, you can see silver plates and a golden goblet containing wine. Everything here shows how rich the family is – the clothes, tableware and even the exotic family pets, the monkey and the parrot.

**A banquet in the fifteenth century.
Up until the 1500s, everyone ate
from trenchers made of bread.**

In those days, people in Britain did not use forks. Instead they cut their meat with a sharp knife, like the ones in the picture (right) and then ate it with their fingers. They dipped the meat into bowls containing different sauces. Since everyone's fingers went into the same bowls, it was very bad manners to eat with dirty fingers or to scratch yourself at the table.

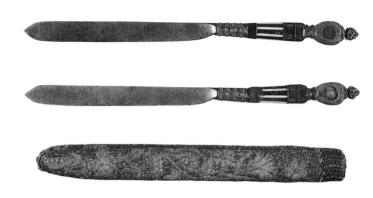

Knives like these, from 1638, were used for eating and were carried in cases like the one at the bottom.

Tom Coryate was an English traveller who visited Italy in 1600. He was amazed to see people eating with forks:

" The reason they use them is that the Italian cannot bear to have his dish touched by fingers, seeing that all men are not alike clean. "

Coryate thought that forks were a good idea and brought some back to England. His friends were not so sure. If you are used to eating with your fingers, it is very tricky learning to use a fork. If you're not careful you might stab yourself in the face! Forks did not catch on widely until the 1750s.

Lord Cobham and his family at their dessert of fruit and nuts.

Alehouses, taverns and inns

Every village had an alehouse, a small cottage where poor people could warm themselves by the fire and drink ale. Alehouses were often run by women, who were called 'alewives'.

Alewives made the ale themselves, out of barley, yeast and water. This is Eleanour Rumming, a well-known Tudor alewife. The picture comes from a poem about her by John Skelton.

Eleanour Rumming.

In the 1500s, people began to drink beer, a drink made from hops and malt as well as barley. Hops made beer last longer than ale, but they also gave it a bitter taste. It took a long time for people to get to like the new drink.

Inns were places where you could eat and sleep as well as drink. They were often built at roadsides in the country and at crossroads, so travellers on long journeys could stop and rest in them. Many old inns can still be seen all over Britain, like the Star Inn at Alfriston in Sussex, which has been serving people for five hundred years. Fynes Morison described what it was like arriving at an English inn:

> "As soon as a passenger comes to an Inn, the servants run to him – one takes his horse, another gives him his room and lights his fire, the third pulls off his boots and cleans them. Then the Host or Hostess visits him, and if he wants to eat with the Host, or at a table with others, his meal will cost him sixpence."

A seventeenth-century painting of wine drinkers relaxing in a tavern.

Above you can see a tavern, a place where wine was sold. The wine had to be brought across the sea, in barrels like the one in the picture, and so it cost much more than ale. British people liked sweet wine, so they usually added sugar to it.

The Star Inn at Alfriston.

New foods from overseas

In the 1500s, European ships set off on long voyages of exploration. They found many lands where different foods were eaten. The explorers brought some of these foods back to Europe.

Lots of the new foods came from America. In America, many plants were eaten which were unknown in Europe. These included potatoes and maize. There was also a strange-looking bird which was eaten in Mexico.

These birds were taken to Europe by Spaniards, who had conquered Mexico in 1519–21. The birds came to Britain in a roundabout way. They were brought by merchants who traded with Turkey. The merchants picked up the birds in Spain on their way from Turkey to Britain. British people did not realize that the birds came from Mexico. They called them 'Turkey cocks', or turkeys.

Potatoes (right), from South America, became very popular in Ireland, Scotland and Wales. English people didn't like potatoes at first. They said that they caused diseases like leprosy and that they should only be fed to animals.

A turkey.

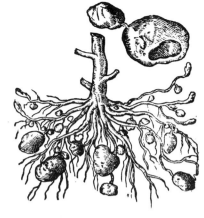

The new plant which was most popular in England was tobacco from North America. Tobacco sellers claimed that smoking was good for you; they said it could cure colds and diseases of the lungs! King James I did not agree. He wrote a pamphlet in which he said that smoking was 'a custom loathsome to the eye, hateful to the nose, harmful to the brain, and dangerous to the lungs'.

However, James could not stop people smoking tobacco. Soon the habit was so popular that some churches had to put up 'no smoking' signs. In the picture below, Stuart men are smoking tobacco in pipes.

A drawing of potatoes, made in 1633.

Timeline

1492
Christopher Columbus sails to the Americas.

1519–21
Spaniards conquer Mexico. They send turkeys and chocolate back to Europe.

1532
Spaniards conquer Peru, where they find potatoes.

1565
Sir John Hawkins brings tobacco to Britain.

1586
Sir Francis Drake brings potatoes to Britain, from the Caribbean.

Tobacco smokers in the early seventeenth century.

Stuart recipes

Cookery books became very popular in the 1650s. They were written for and by wealthy ladies who wanted to keep up to date with the latest ways of cooking food. These books, like the one on the right, can tell us a lot about the sort of food that people ate. They show that English people were getting interested in foreign ways of preparing food. Recipes often appear with 'After the French Fashion' written above them.

A Stuart recipe book.

We can also find out a lot about food from diaries. The most famous diary of the time was written by Samuel Pepys (pronounced Peeps). Pepys was always interested in trying out new kinds of food, and his diary is full of descriptions of meals.

A portrait of Samuel Pepys by John Closterman.

On 10 February 1669, Pepys had dinner with James, Duke of York, the younger brother of King Charles II. Pepys wrote about a new sauce which the Duke had discovered — the Spanish ambassador had shown him how to make it:

> *" He mightily praised his sauce which he did then eat with everything, and said it was the best sauce in the world. It is made of some parsley and dry toast, beat together with vinegar, salt and a little pepper. He eats it with flesh or fowl or fish. I did like the notion of the sauce and by and by did taste it, and liked it mightily. "*

Pestle

Mortar

You could try making this sauce yourself. The Duke made his sauce in a mortar, like the one in the picture. He mashed up the ingredients with a pestle. If you don't have a pestle and mortar, you could use a bowl and a spoon.

A pestle and mortar.

The first hot drinks

In the late 1600s, English people began to drink new hot drinks from overseas. The merchants who sold the new drinks claimed that they could cure many different illnesses. At first, people drank them for their health, or just to see what they were like. Later they began to like the taste of them.

The first drink to catch on was coffee. This was brought to England from North Africa via Turkey, and sold in special coffee houses. A French traveller called François Misson visited a coffee house in the 1690s. He explained why the English liked going to them :

> *"You have all manner of news there. You have a good fire, which you may sit by as long as you please. You have a dish of coffee. You meet your friends, and all for a penny if you don't care to spend more. "*

A London coffee house in 1668. The men are reading 'news sheets', an early form of newspaper.

You can see in the picture above that coffee houses were used by men rather than women. They went there to chat and to do business. Different coffee houses were used by different groups: politicians, writers, actors and bankers all had their own special coffee houses.

As well as lots of coffee houses, London had two special chocolate houses – *White's* and the *Cocoa Tree*. They served chocolate as a hot drink, mixed with water and, later, milk. Chocolate came from America and was more expensive than coffee. It was mostly drunk by rich people. Look at the advert for milk chocolate. It says that the drink was recommended by physicians (doctors).

Timeline

1650

The first English coffee house opens, in Oxford.

1657

Tea, from China, is first sold in England.

1693

White's, the first chocolate house, opens in London.

Sold Here
Sir Hans Sloane's
Milk Chocolate
Made (only) by William White, *Succeſsor to* Mr. Nicholas Sanders, No. 8 *Greek Street, Soho*, London.

Greatly recommended by ſeveral eminent Physicians eſpecially those of *Sir Hans Sloane's* Acquaintance, for its Lightneſs on the Stomach, & its great Uſe in all Conſumptive Caſes.

What is not ſigned with my Name and ſealed with my Arms, is Counterfeit.

An advert for milk chocolate from the early eighteenth century.

Tea, which came from China, was made fashionable by Charles II's Portuguese wife, Catherine. At first, it was most popular with wealthy women. In the 1700s, people started drinking tea instead of ale for breakfast. Tea eventually became the most popular drink in England.

27

Timeline

1480	1500	1520	1540	1560	1580

Tudors

1485 HENRY VII

1509 HENRY VIII

1547 EDWARD VI

1553 MARY TUDOR

1558 ELIZABETH I

1480–1500	1500–1520	1520–1540	1540–1560	1560–1580	1580–1600

1480–1500

1492
Christopher Columbus sails to the Americas.

1498
Vasco da Gama sails to India, in search of spices.

1500–1520

1509
John Cabot tries to sail round the north of Canada.

1519–21
Spaniards conquer Mexico. They send turkeys and chocolate back to Europe.

1520–1540

1524
Hops, for beer-making, are first grown in Kent.

1532
Spaniards conquer Peru, where they find potatoes.

1534
Henry VIII becomes Head of the Church in England and Wales.

1536
Henry VIII's second wife, Anne Boleyn, is put to death.

1536–39
Henry VIII has the monasteries destroyed.

1540–1560

1543
The Belgian-born scientist Andreas Vesalius publishes his book about the human body.

1547–53
Many schools and colleges are built.

1549
Robert Kett leads a rebellion in Norfolk.

1553–58
Protestants are persecuted and put to death.

1560–1580

1565
Sir John Hawkins brings tobacco to Britain.

1567
As a Catholic, Mary Queen of Scots flees from Scotland but is imprisoned in England.

1577
Sir Francis Drake sets off on his voyage around the world.

1580–1600

1586
Potatoes are brought to Britain and Ireland from the Caribbean. They become popular in Ireland.

1587
Mary Queen of Scots is executed.

1588
The Spanish Armada is defeated.

1595
Sir Walter Raleigh explores South America.

1590–1616
William Shakespeare writes his plays.

1600   1620   1640   1660   1680   1700

Stuarts

1603 JAMES I (JAMES VI OF SCOTLAND)

1625 CHARLES I

1649–1660 COMMONWEALTH
1653 OLIVER CROMWELL
1658 RICHARD CROMWELL

1660 CHARLES II

1685 JAMES II
1688 WILLIAM III & MARY II

1702–1714 ANNE

1600–1620	1620–1640	1640–1660	1660–1680	1680–1700	1700–1720
1601 Thomas Coryate brings the first forks to Britain, from Italy. **1606** Dutch bring the first shipment of tea from China to Europe. **1607** The English found a settlement, Jamestown, in North America. **1610** The explorer Henry Hudson discovers a huge bay in northern Canada. It is named after him. **1620** The Puritan Pilgrim Fathers sail from England to settle in America.	**1628** The scientist William Harvey describes how blood goes round the body. **1630–41** Charles I rules without Parliament. **1640** The English start to grow sugar-cane in Barbados, in the West Indies.	**1642** The Civil War begins. **1649** Charles I is executed. **1650** The first English coffee house opens, in Oxford. **1652** Chocolate, from America, is first brought to England. **1657** Tea, from China, is first sold in England. **1660** The Restoration of the monarchy. Charles II becomes king.	**1660s** Forks begin to become popular in Britain among wealthy people. **1660–69** Samuel Pepys writes his diary. **1660–85** Scientists Robert Hooke and Isaac Newton study light and gravity. **1660–1700** Coffee houses become popular. **1665** The plague. **1666** The Great Fire of London.	**1690** The Battle of the Boyne in Ireland. **1694** Queen Mary dies. **1700** English East India Company sets up a trading base in Canton, China, to meet the growing demand in England for tea.	**1707** England and Scotland are officially united.

Glossary

Ambassador An official sent by the government of one country to another.

Coffee house A place selling coffee. Many coffee houses eventually turned into gentlemen's clubs.

Inn A place selling food and drink, where people could spend the night.

News sheet An early form of newspaper.

Ratchet hanger A piece of metal with a jagged edge like a saw. Pots hung from it over a fire.

Roasted Cooked in front of an open fire.

Saint's day A religious festival in memory of a saint. Many saints' days were dropped when Henry VIII made himself Head of the Church.

Spit A long piece of metal on which meat was roasted. Anything from a chicken to a whole ox could be roasted on a spit.

Scurvy A disease caused by going without fresh food.

Tavern A place selling wine.

Welsh oatcakes
You will need:
350g (12 oz) fine oatmeal
1 teaspoon salt
A pinch of bicarbonate of soda
40g (½ oz) butter or margarine
150 ml (¼ pint) water

Ask a grown-up to help you.

◆ Mix the oatmeal, salt and bicarbonate of soda together in a bowl.
◆ In another bowl, cut up the margarine or butter into small pieces.
◆ Ask a grown-up to boil the water and pour it over the margarine or butter – stir until it has melted. Then add it to the oatmeal mix, stirring it in.
◆ Sprinkle a work surface with oatmeal, and turn out the mixture on to it.
◆ Knead the mixture with your fingers until you have a smooth dough.
◆ With a rolling-pin, roll out the dough until it is thin.
◆ Cut the dough into small shapes (circles, triangles or squares) and place them on greased baking sheets.
◆ Ask a grown-up to bake the oatcakes in the oven at 150°C, 300°F or Gas Mark 2, for one hour until crisp.
◆ Put them on a wire rack to cool.
◆ You can eat your oatcakes spread with butter or cream cheese.

Books to read

Peter Brears, *Food and Cooking in 16th Century Britain* (English Heritage, 1985)

Peter Brears, *Food and Cooking in 17th Century Britain* (English Heritage, 1985)

Lisa Chaney, *Investigating Food in History* (The National Trust, 1992)

Helen Edom and Felicity Brooks, *Food and Eating* (Usborne, 1989)

Jo Lawrie, *Pot Luck: Cooking and Recipes from the Past* (A & C Black, 1991)

Gill Tanner and Tim Wood, *Cooking* (A & C Black, 1992)

Places to visit

Throughout Britain there are many Tudor and Stuart houses, complete with kitchens, which are open to the public.

East Riddlesden Hall, Keighley, Yorkshire (tel. 0535 607 075): Seventeenth-century kitchen with equipment.

Buckland Abbey, Yelverton, Devon (tel. 0822 853 607): Elizabethan kitchen with open hearths and a bread oven.

Cotehele Hall, Cornwall (tel. 0579 50434): Fifteenth/sixteenth-century manor house with kitchen and dovecote.

Ham House, near Richmond, Surrey (tel. 081 940 1950): Stuart house with kitchen, larders, bakehouse and a Great Dining Hall.

Hampton Court Palace, Surrey (tel. 081 781 9500): A famous Tudor palace.

Hardwick Hall, Derbyshire (tel. 0246 850 430): The great house of Bess of Hardwick, one of the richest women in Elizabethan England.

Historic Scotland, Edinburgh (tel. 031 244 3102): Phone for information on Stuart houses.

Raglan Castle, Abergavenny, Wales (tel. 0291 690228): Fifteenth-century castle, with buttery, pantry and kitchens.

Index

Words in **bold** are subjects shown in pictures as well as in the text.